Keith & Frances.

Great Piano Classics
Twenty-five world-famous pieces

Kevin Mayhew

We hope you enjoy *Great Piano Classics*.
Further copies are available from your local music shop.

In case of difficulty, please contact the publisher direct:

The Sales Department
KEVIN MAYHEW LTD
Rattlesden
Bury St Edmunds
Suffolk IP30 0SZ

Phone 01449 737978
Fax 01449 737834

Please ask for our complete catalogue of outstanding Instrumental Music.

Front Cover: *A vase of rich summer flowers* by Jan van Huysum (1682-1749).
Reproduced by kind permission of Fine Art Photographic Library, London.

Cover designed by Juliette Clarke and Graham Johnstone.
Picture Research: Jane Rayson.

First published in Great Britain in 1994 by Kevin Mayhew Ltd.

© Copyright 1994 Kevin Mayhew Ltd.

ISBN 0 86209 510 7
Catalogue No: 3611111

The music in this book is protected by copyright and may not be reproduced in
any way for sale or private use without the consent of the copyright owner.

Printed and bound in Great Britain.

Contents

		Page
Adagio from 'Moonlight' Sonata	Ludwig van Beethoven	61
Adagio from 'Pathétique' Sonata	Ludwig van Beethoven	45
Anitra's Dance from 'Peer Gynt'	Edvard Grieg	32
Cavatina (Song Without Words Op 102 No 6)	Felix Mendelssohn	30
Chanson Triste Op 40 No 2	Peter Ilyich Tchaikovsky	39
Clair de Lune	Claude Debussy	52
Consolation No 5	Franz Liszt	36
Dreaming from 'Scenes of Childhood'	Robert Schumann	58
First Loss from 'Album for the Young'	Robert Schumann	14
Für Elise	Ludwig van Beethoven	18
Gymnopédie I	Erik Satie	69
Humoreske Op 101 No 7	Antonín Dvořák	10
Lullaby Op 39 No 15	Johannes Brahms	50
Meditation (Song Without Words Op 30 No 3)	Felix Mendelssohn	16
Moment Musical No 3	Franz Schubert	78
Prelude in A	Frédéric Chopin	60
Prelude in B minor	Frédéric Chopin	24
Prelude in C	Johann Sebastian Bach	5
Prelude in C minor	Johann Sebastian Bach	66
Prelude in E minor	Frédéric Chopin	76
Reverie Op 39 No 21	Peter Ilyich Tchaikovsky	72
Salut d'Amour	Edward Elgar	26
Solfeggietto	Carl Philipp Emanuel Bach	42
The Girl with the Flaxen Hair	Claude Debussy	74
To a Wild Rose	Edward MacDowell	8

PRELUDE IN C

Johann Sebastian Bach (1685-1750)

© Copyright 1994 by Kevin Mayhew Ltd.
It is illegal to photocopy music.

TO A WILD ROSE
Edward MacDowell (1860-1908)

© Copyright 1994 by Kevin Mayhew Ltd.
It is illegal to photocopy music.

HUMORESKE

Antonín Dvořák (1841-1904)

© Copyright 1994 by Kevin Mayhew Ltd.
It is illegal to photocopy music.

rit.
a tempo
fz
pp
staccato
rit.

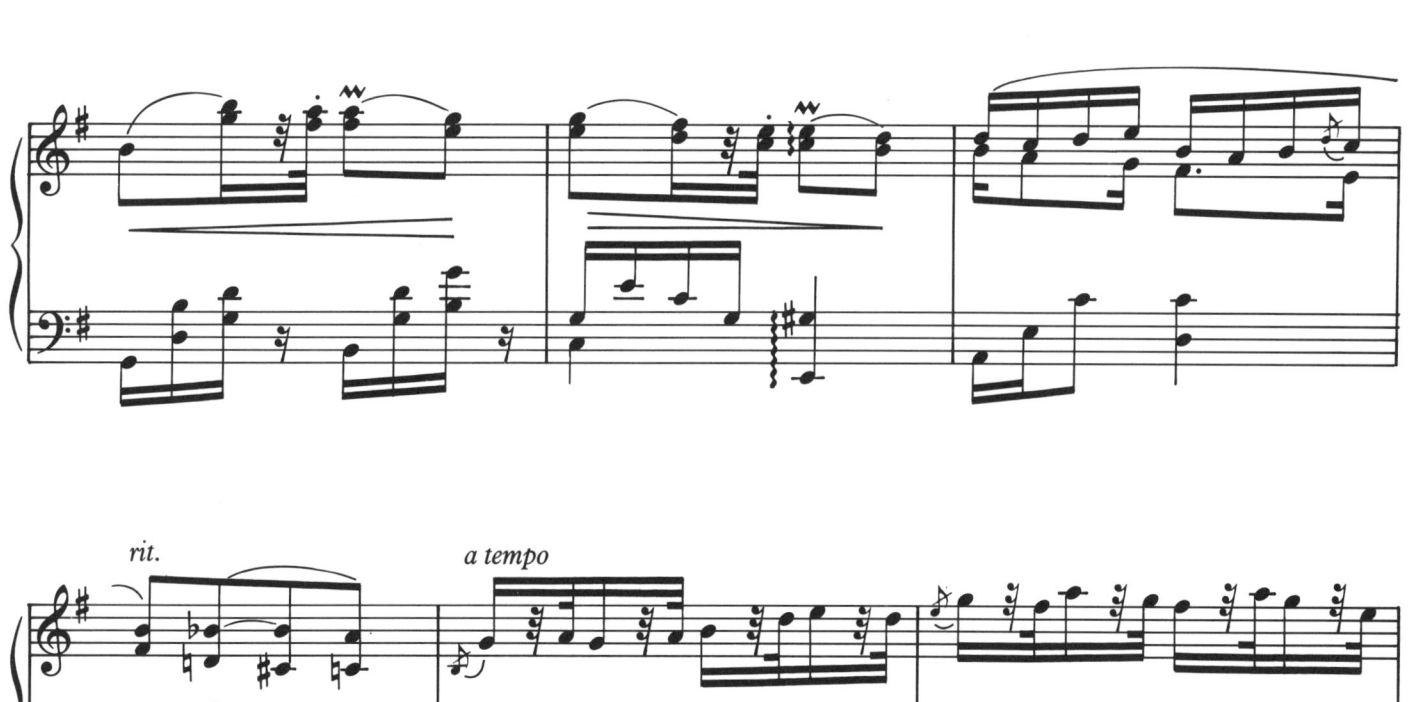

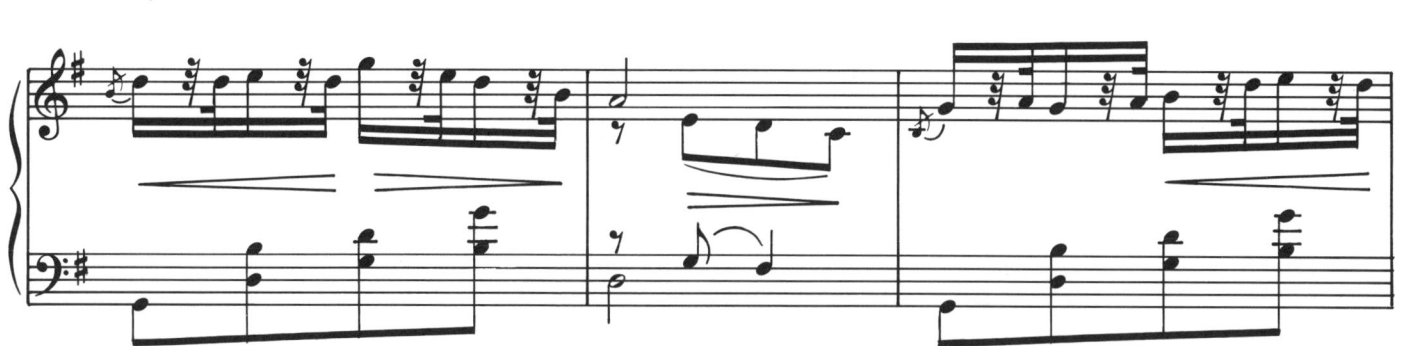

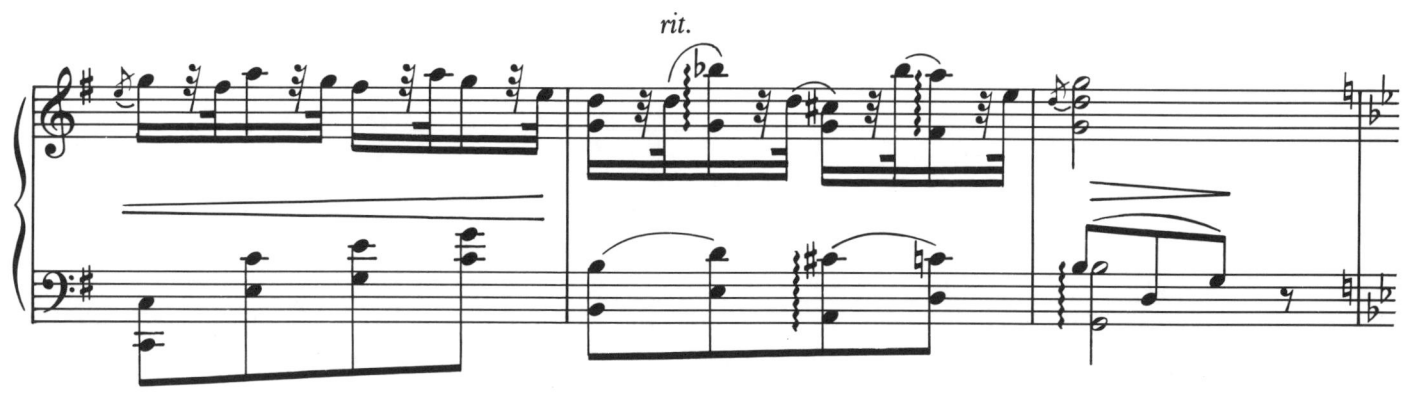

FIRST LOSS

Robert Schumann (1810-1856)

MEDITATION

Felix Mendelssohn (1809-1847)

© Copyright 1994 by Kevin Mayhew Ltd.
It is illegal to photocopy music.

FÜR ELISE

Ludwig van Beethoven (1770-1827)

© Copyright 1994 by Kevin Mayhew Ltd.
It is illegal to photocopy music.

PRELUDE IN B MINOR

Frédéric Chopin (1810-1849)

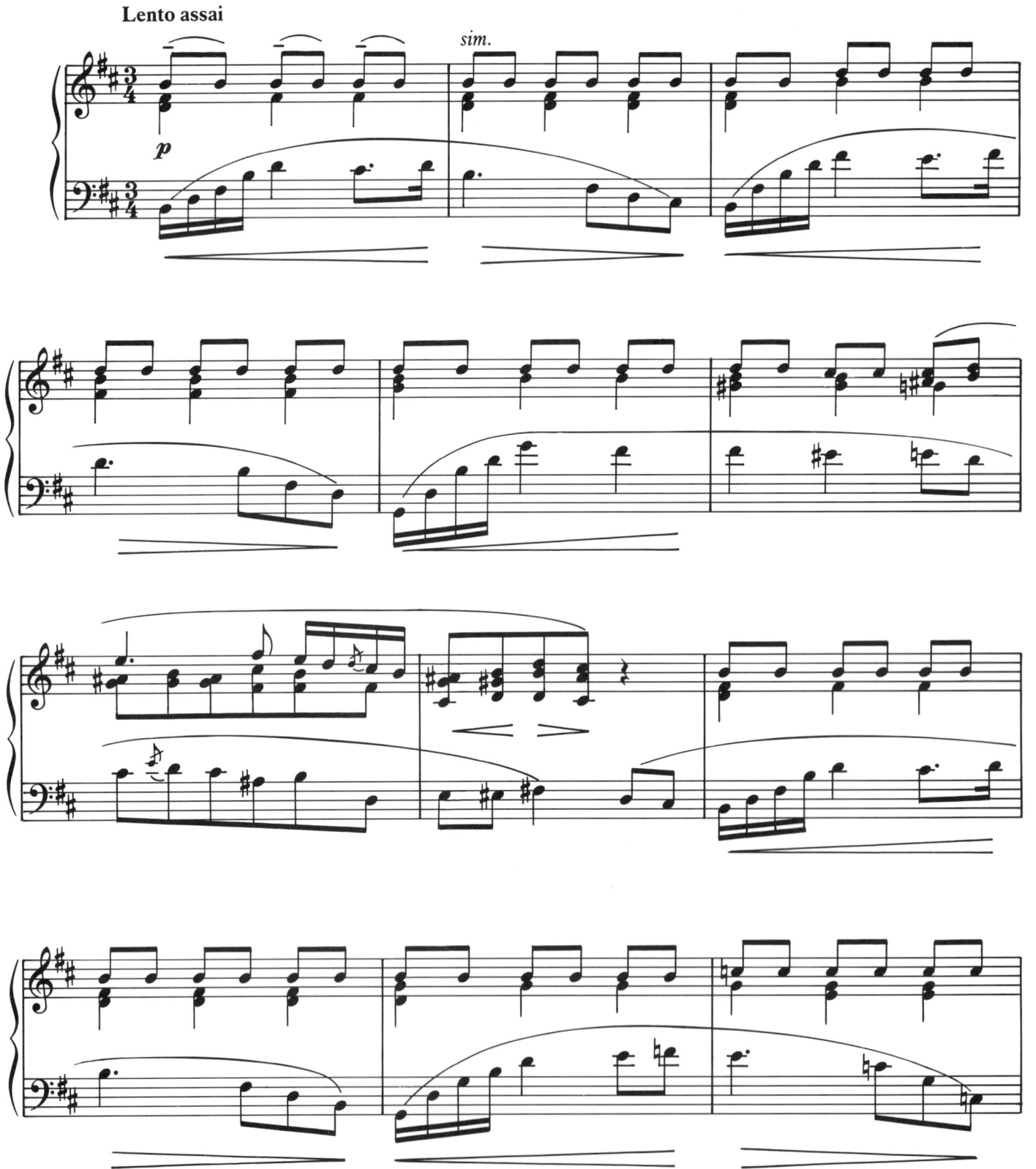

© Copyright 1994 by Kevin Mayhew Ltd.
It is illegal to photocopy music.

SALUT D'AMOUR

Edward Elgar (1857-1934)

© Copyright 1994 by Kevin Mayhew Ltd.
It is illegal to photocopy music.

CAVATINA

Felix Mendelssohn (1809-1847)

ANITRA'S DANCE
Edvard Grieg (1843-1907)

CONSOLATION
Franz Liszt (1811-1886)

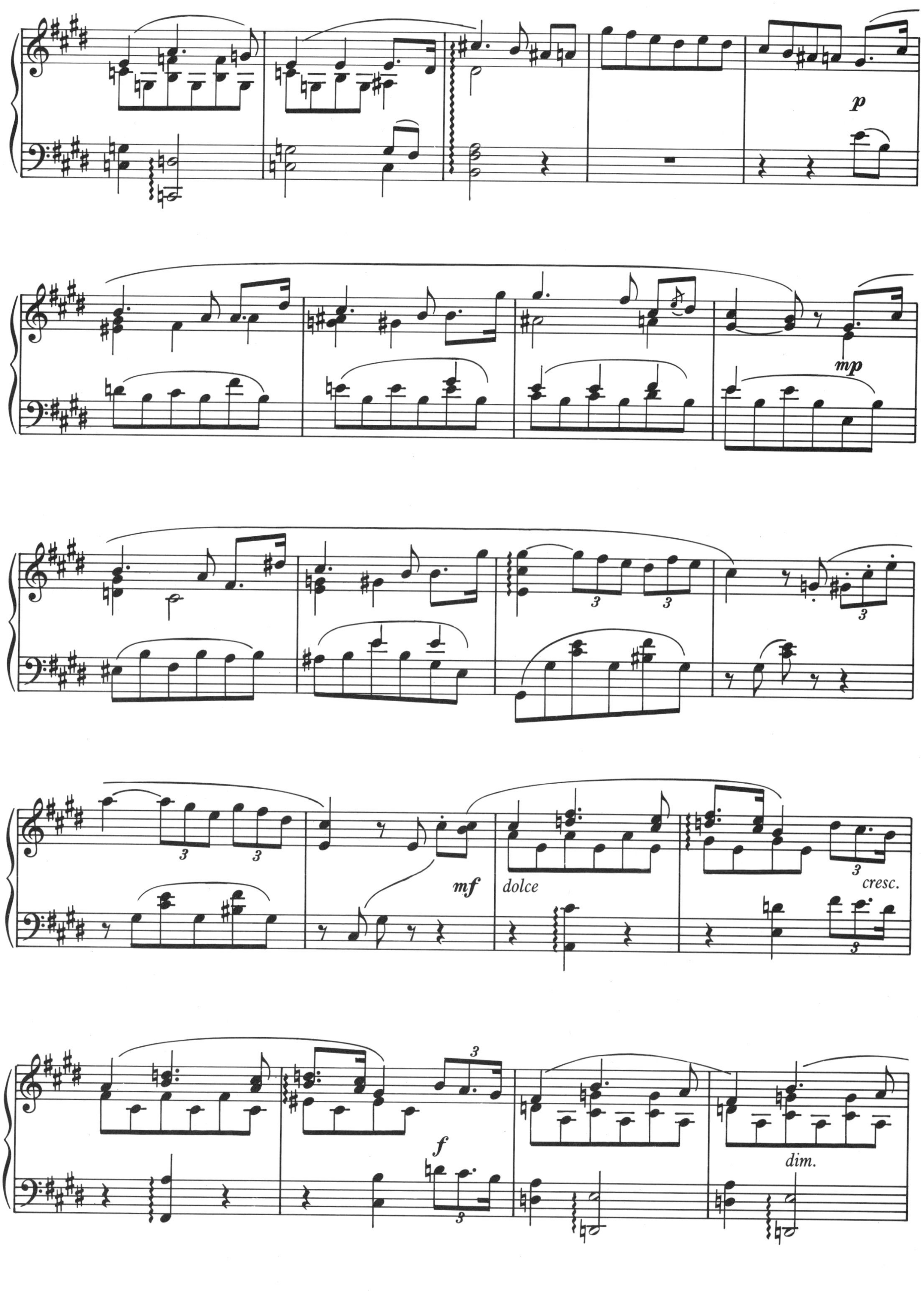
p
mp
mf
dolce
cresc.
f
dim.

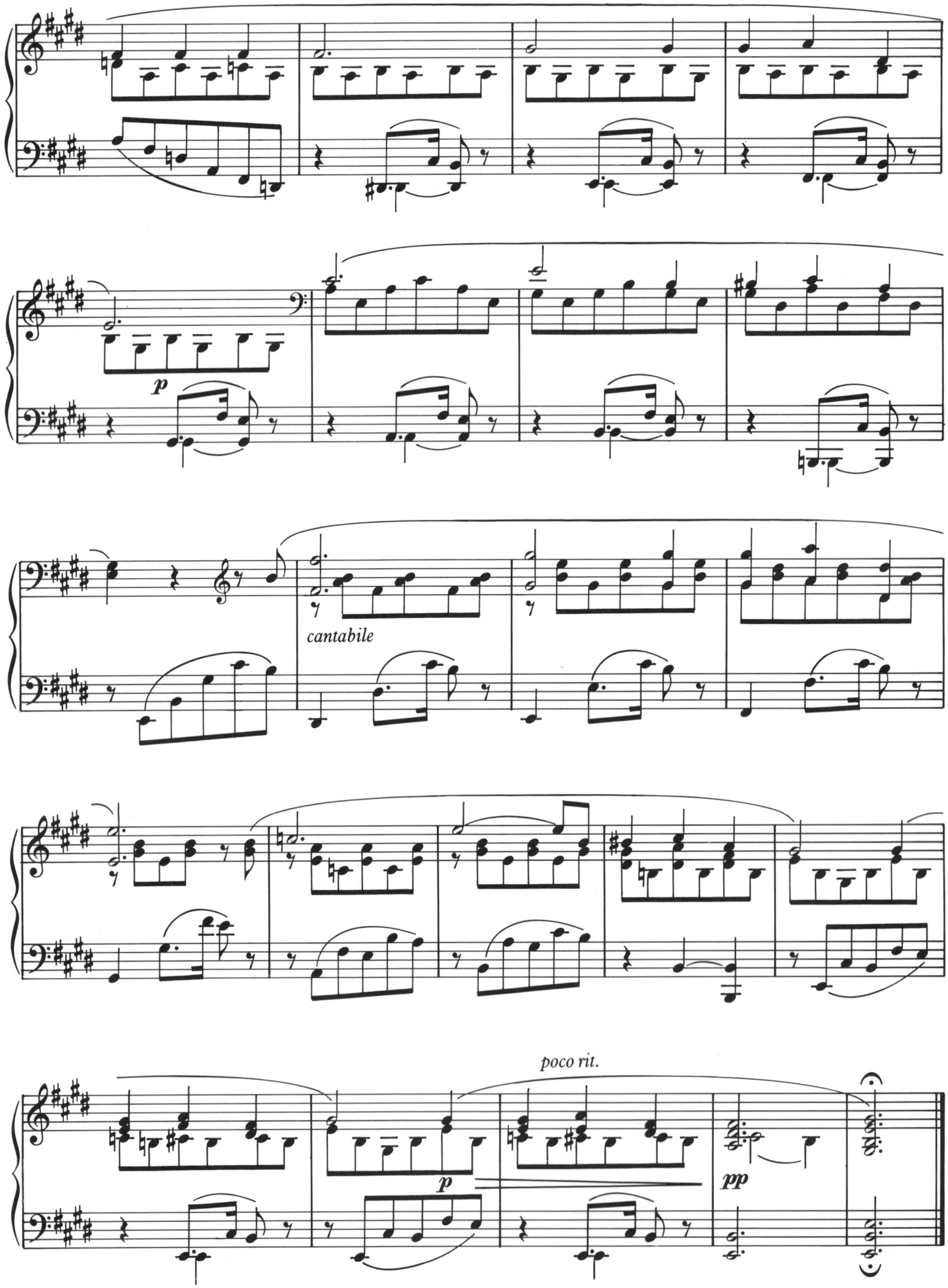
p
cantabile
poco rit.
p
pp

CHANSON TRISTE

Peter Ilyich Tchaikovsky (1840-1893)

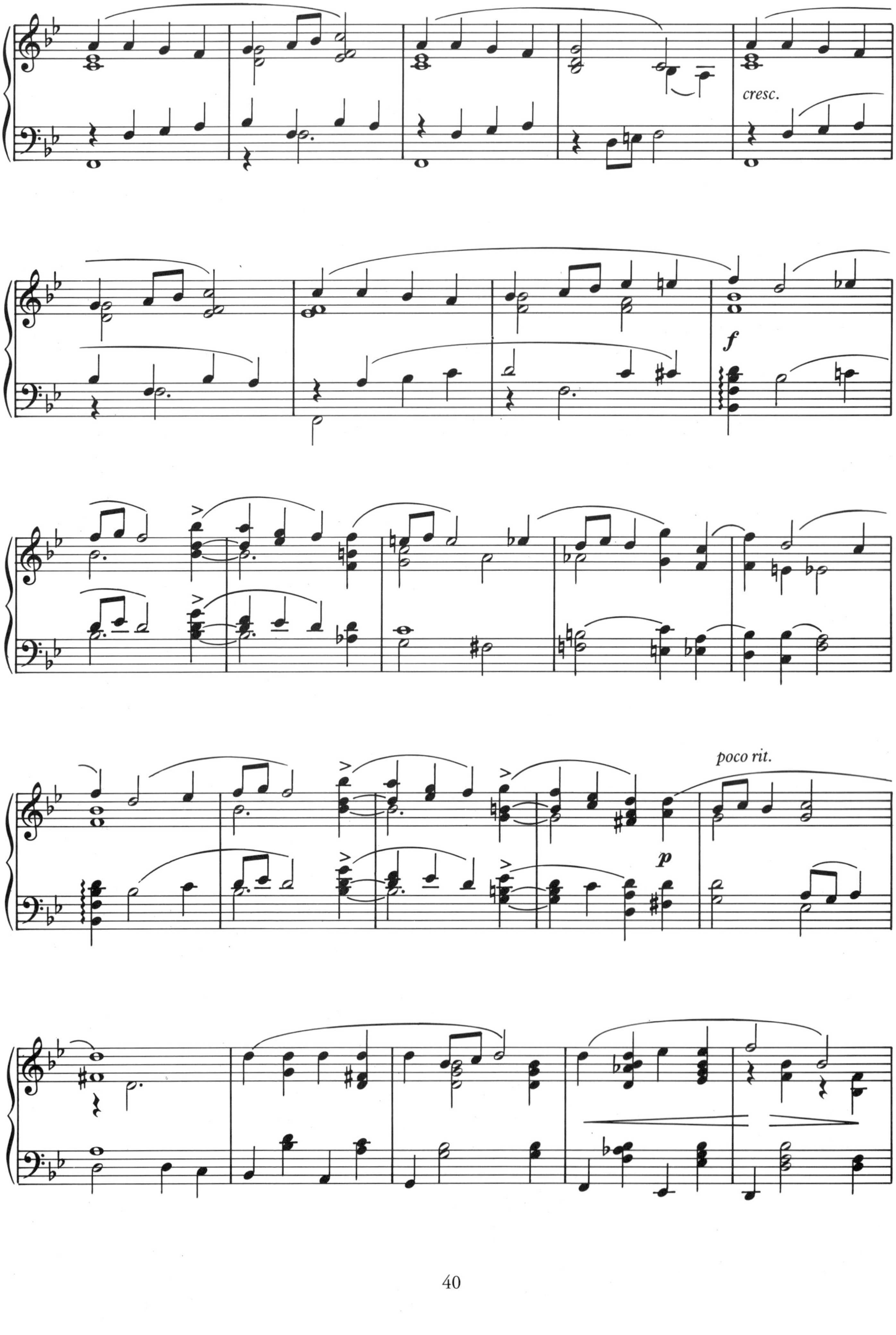
cresc.
f
poco rit.
p

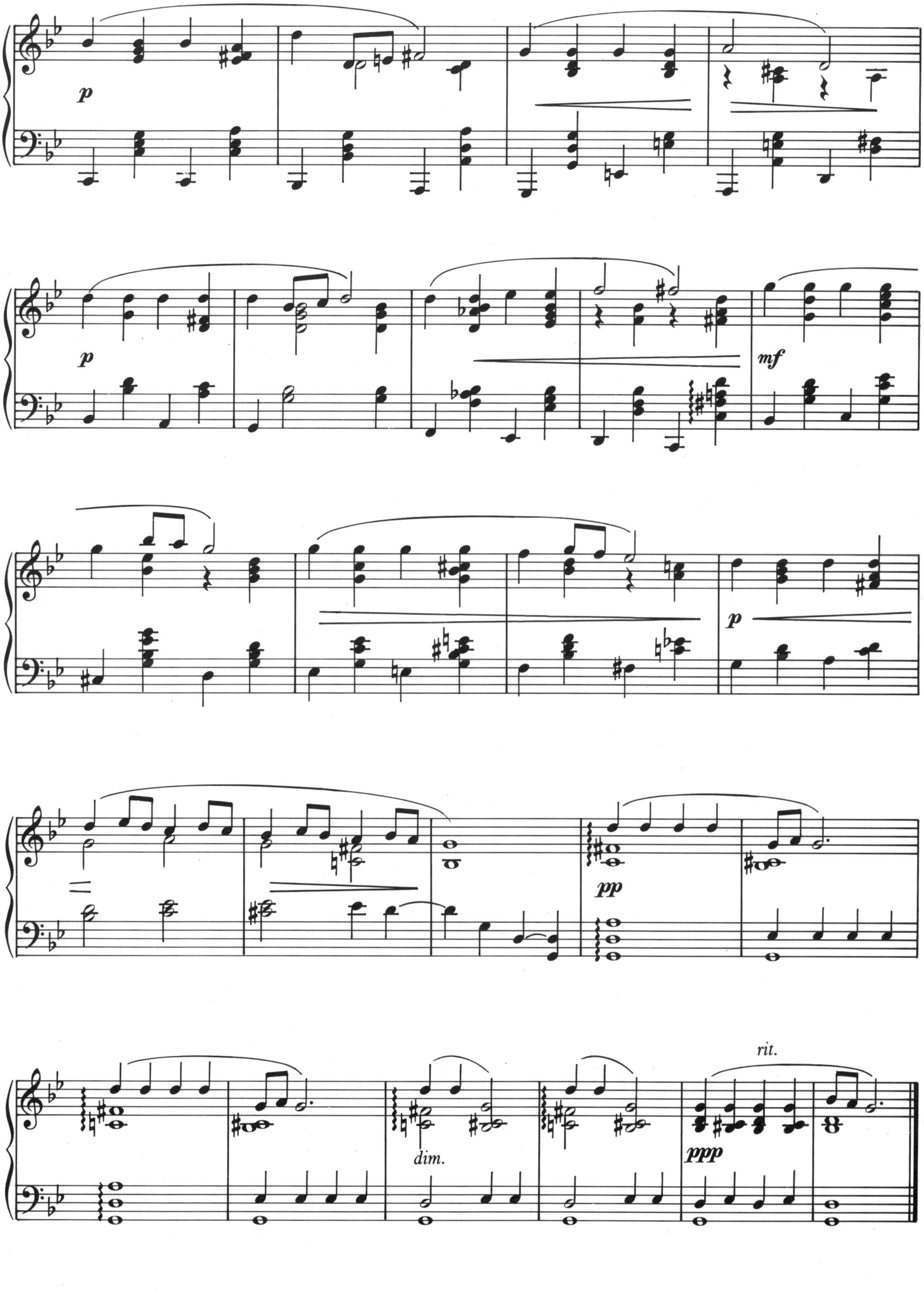
p
p
mf
p
pp
dim.
rit.
ppp

SOLFEGGIETTO

Carl Philipp Emanuel Bach (1714-1788)

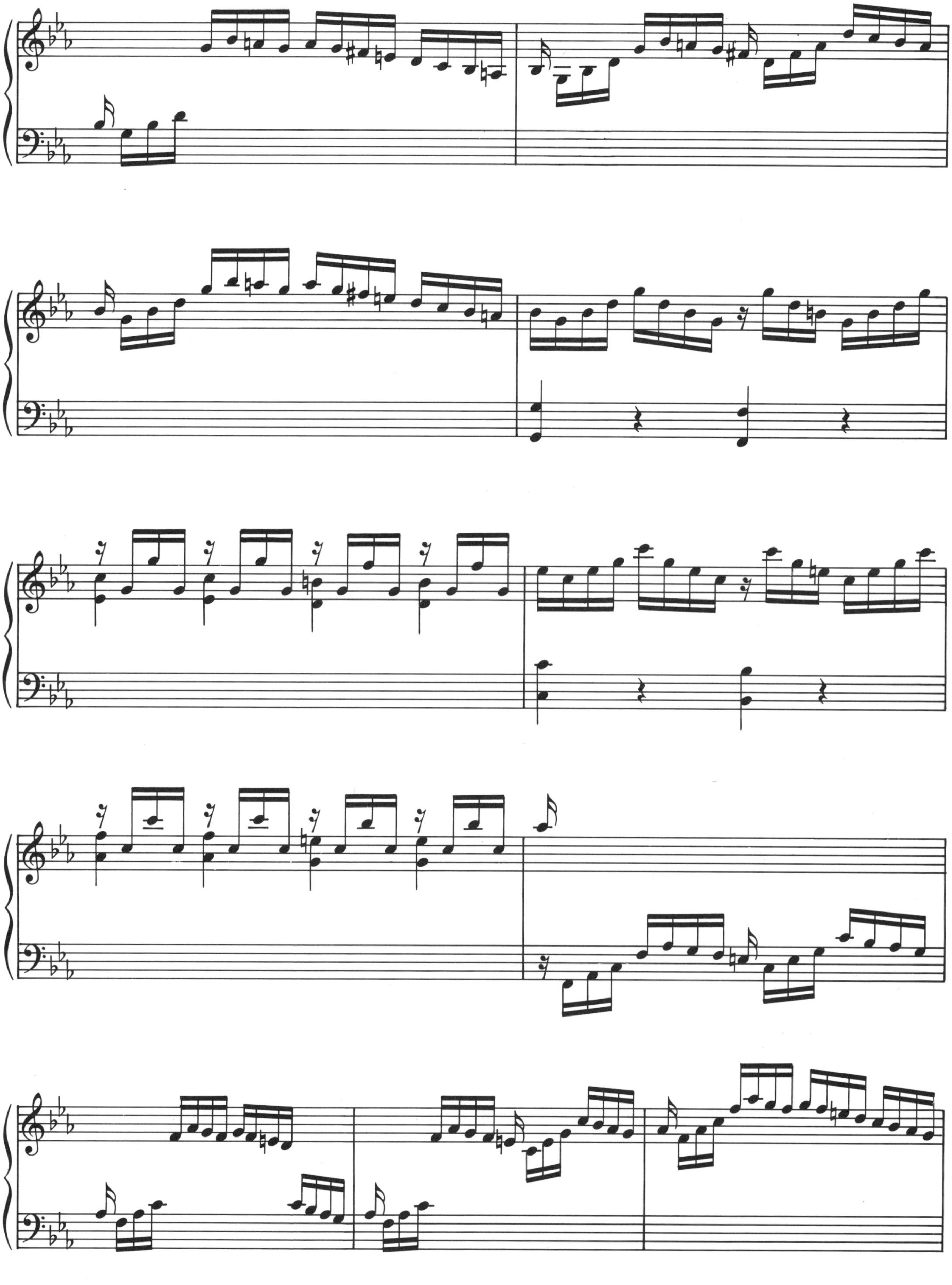

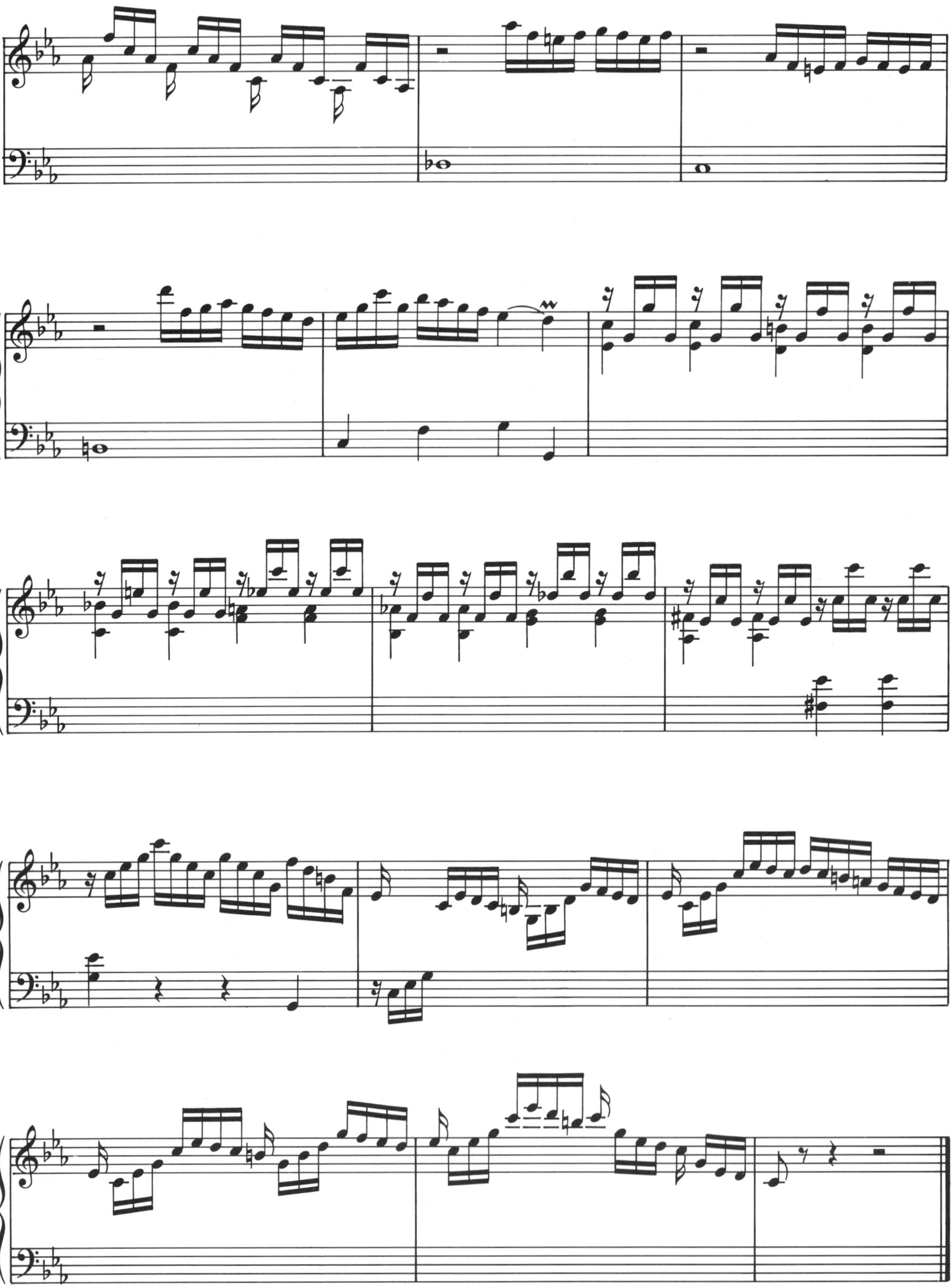

ADAGIO from 'Pathétique' Sonata

Ludwig van Beethoven (1770-1827)

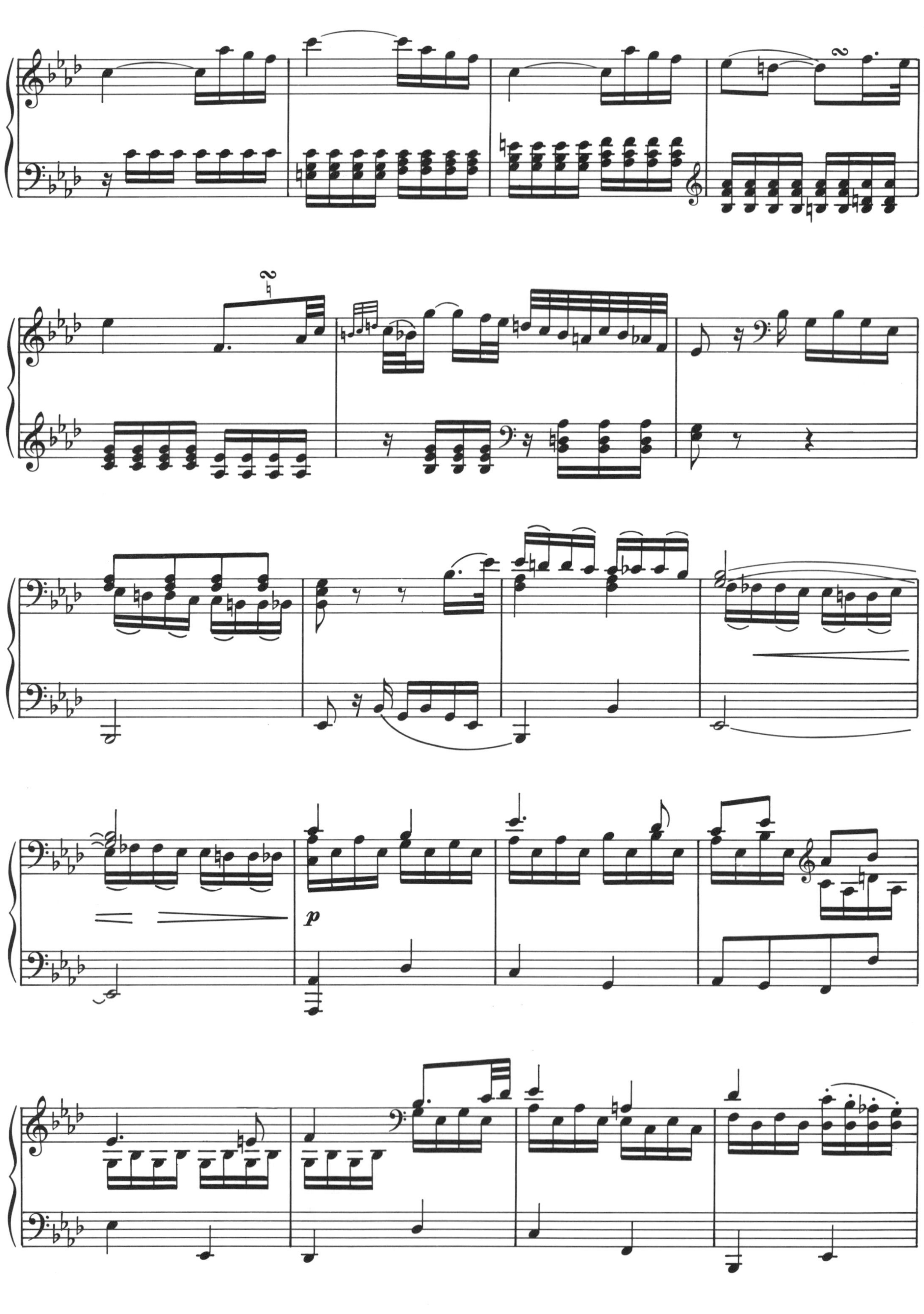
p

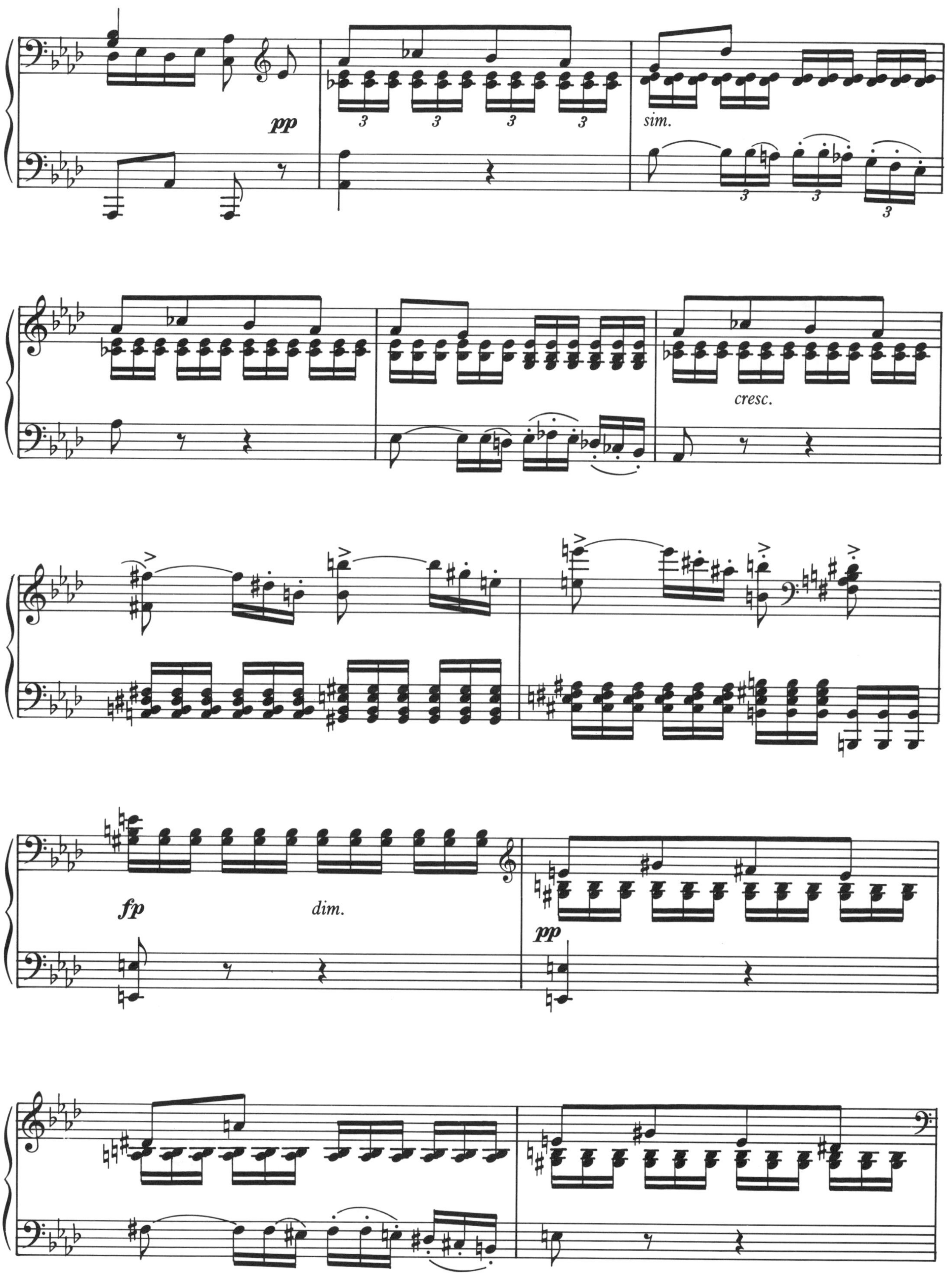
pp
sim.
cresc.
fp
dim.
pp

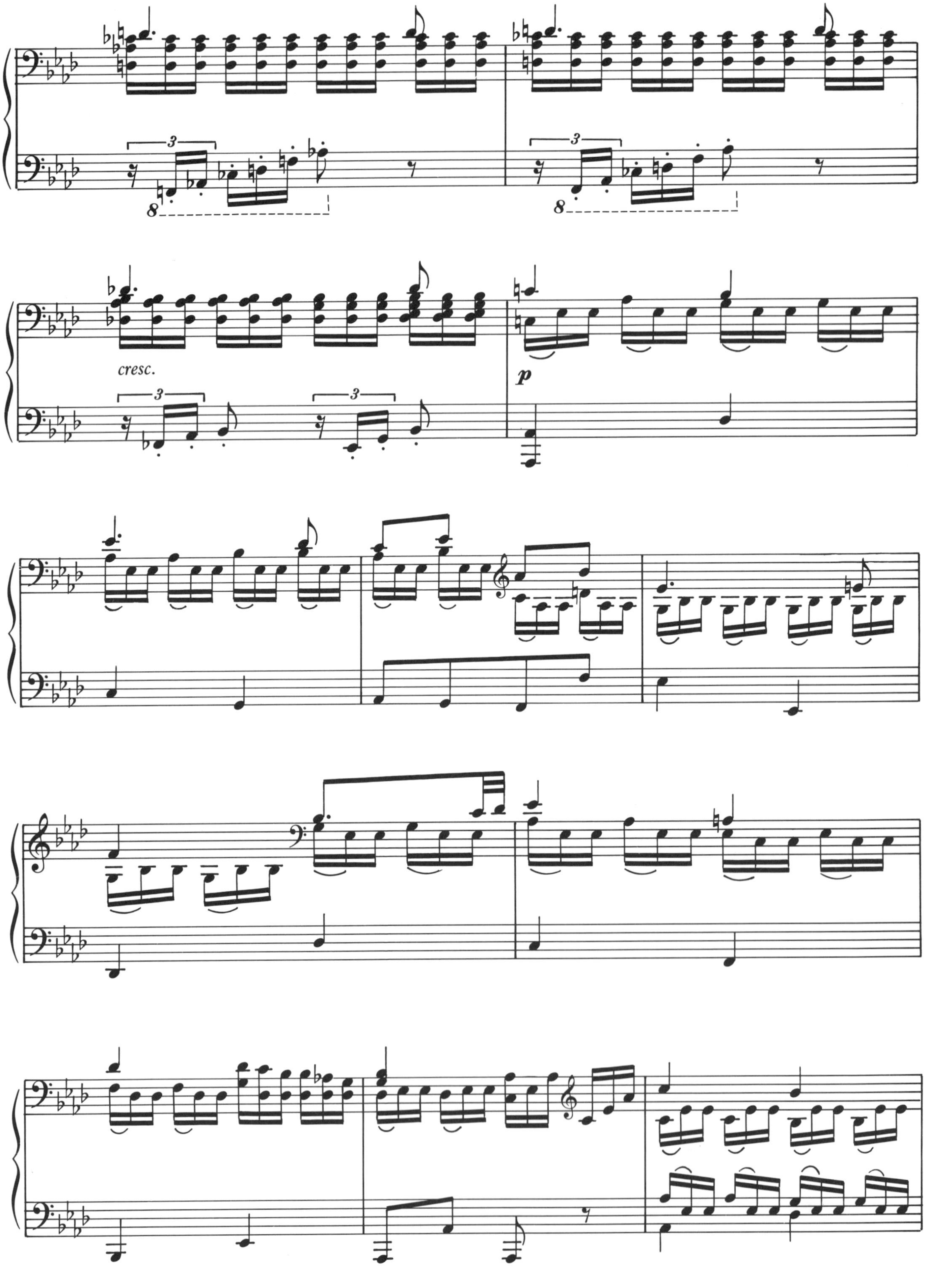
cresc.
p

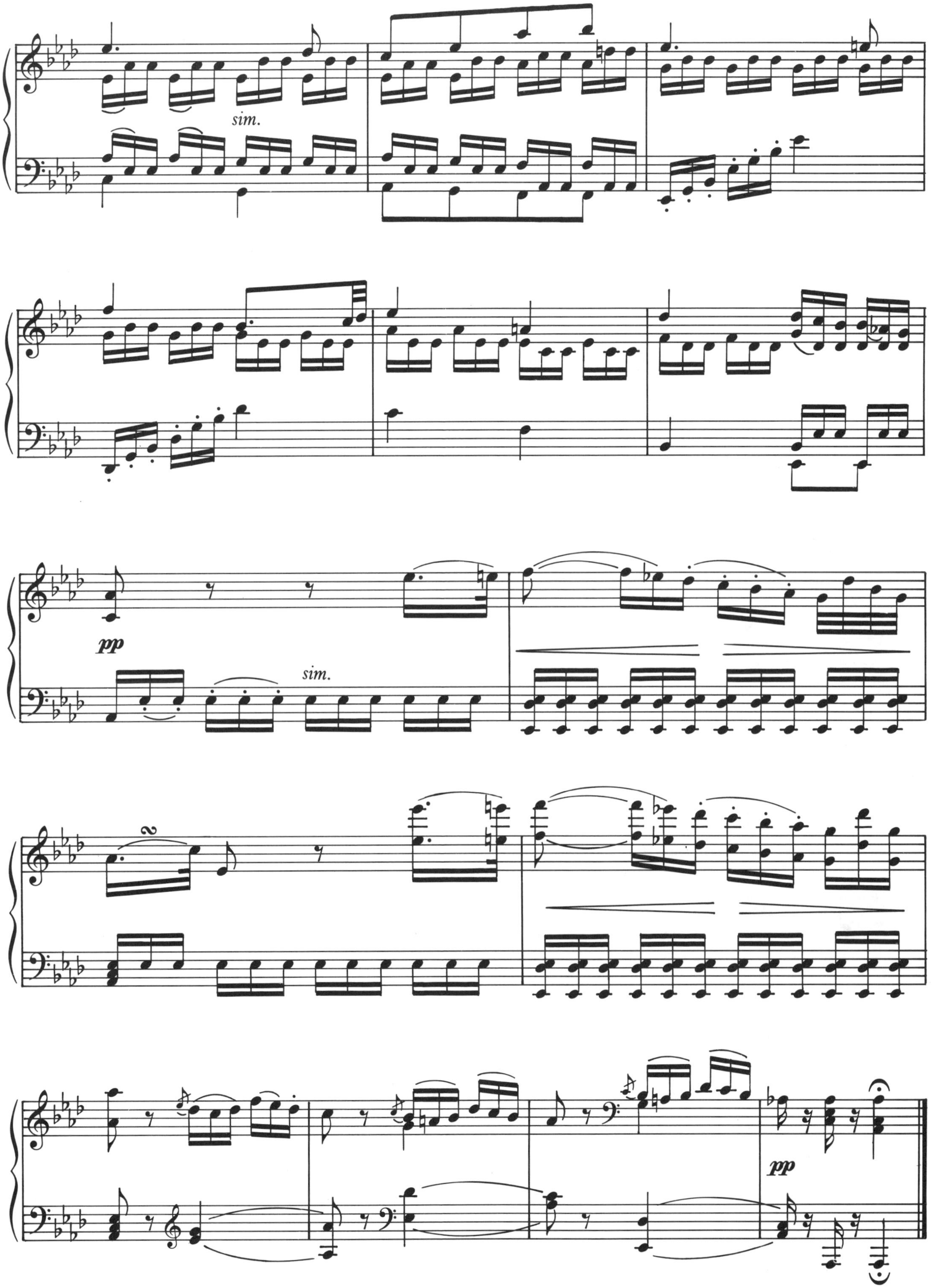
sim.
pp
sim.
pp

LULLABY

Johannes Brahms (1833-1897)

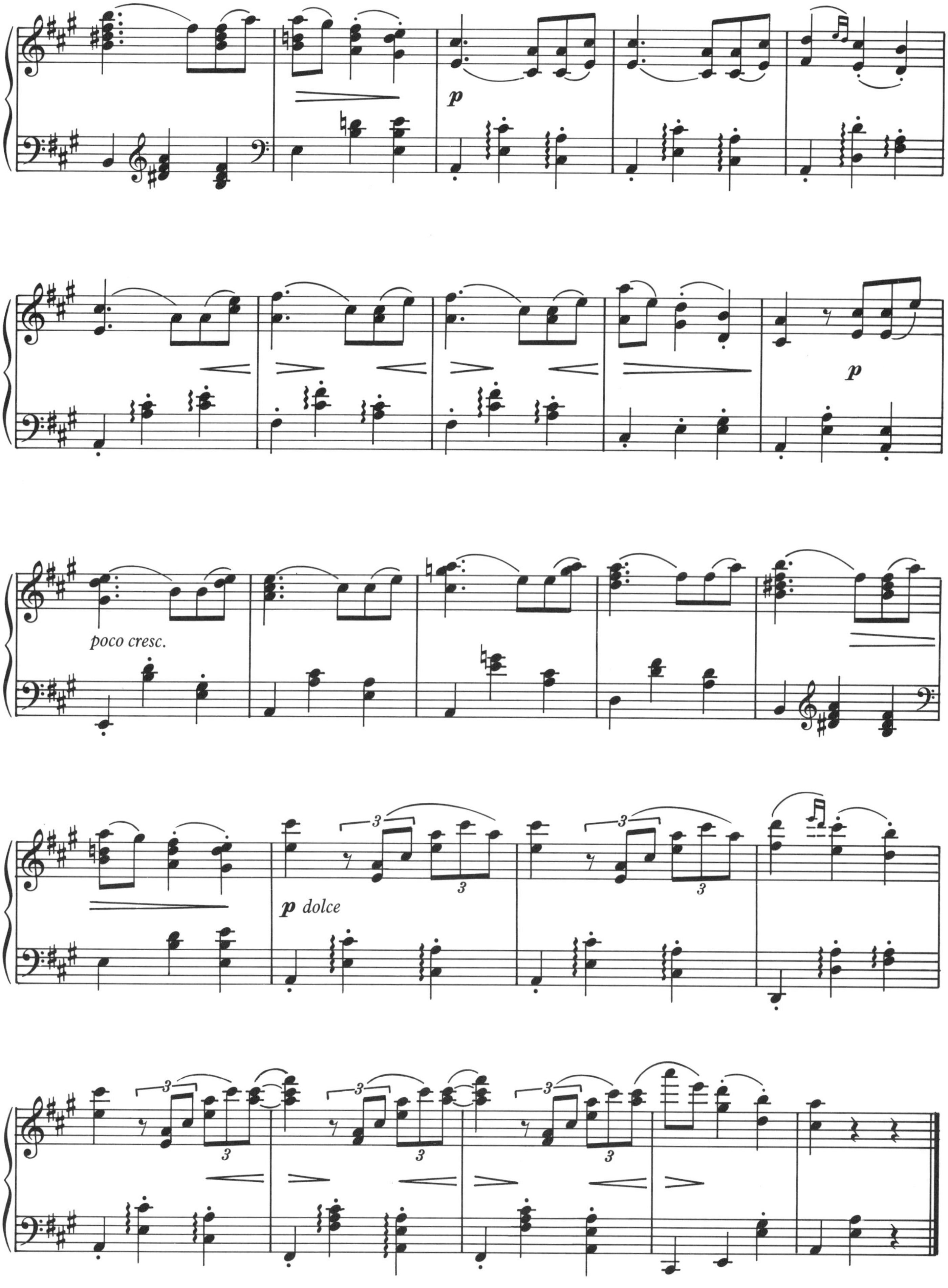
p
p
poco cresc.
p dolce

CLAIR DE LUNE

Claude Debussy (1862-1918)

Andante espressivo

pp

© Copyright 1994 by Kevin Mayhew Ltd.
It is illegal to photocopy music.

Tempo rubato

pp

poco a poco più animato

cresc. poco a poco

dim.

Poco più mosso

pp

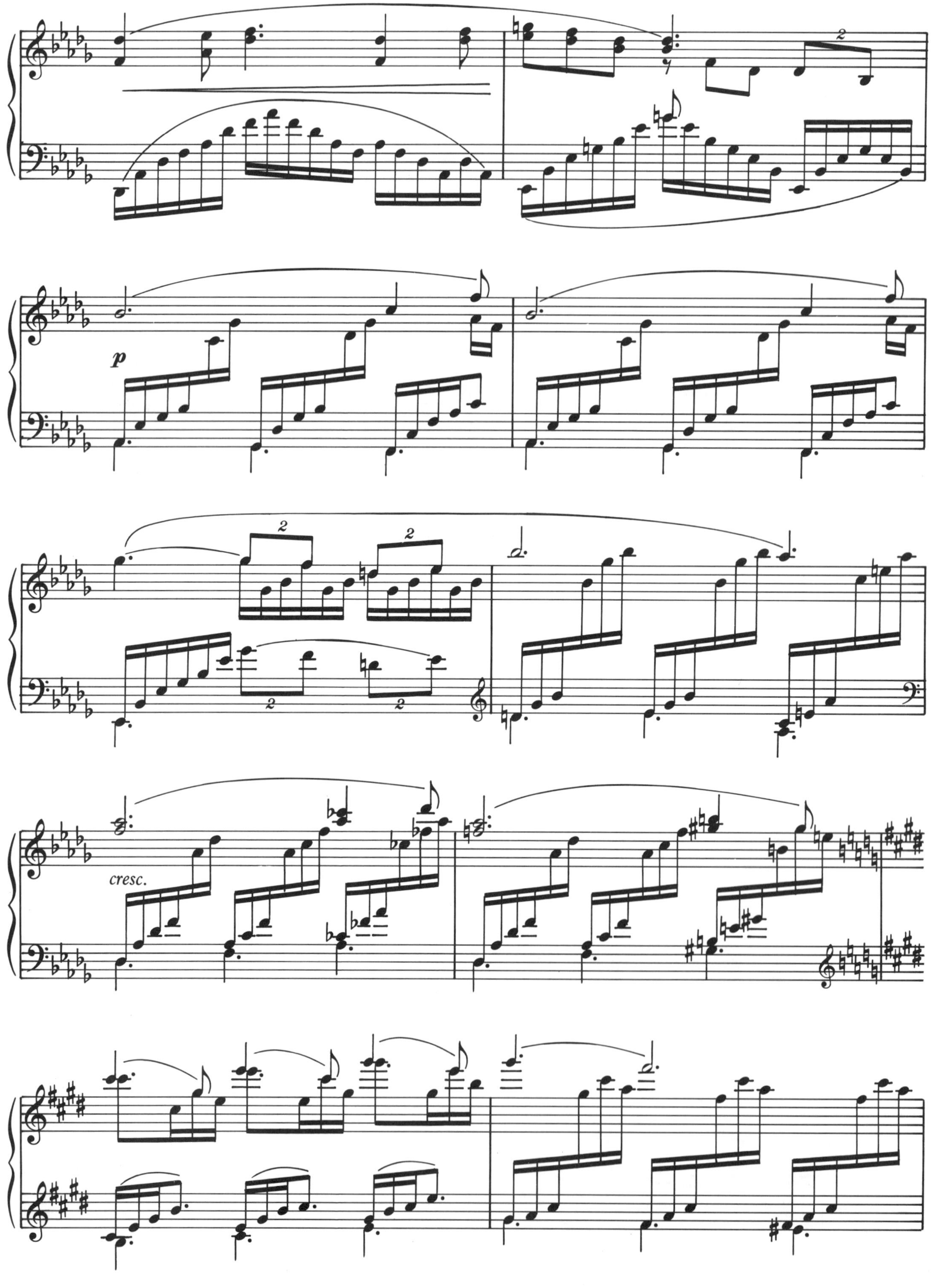
2
p
2
2
2
2
cresc.

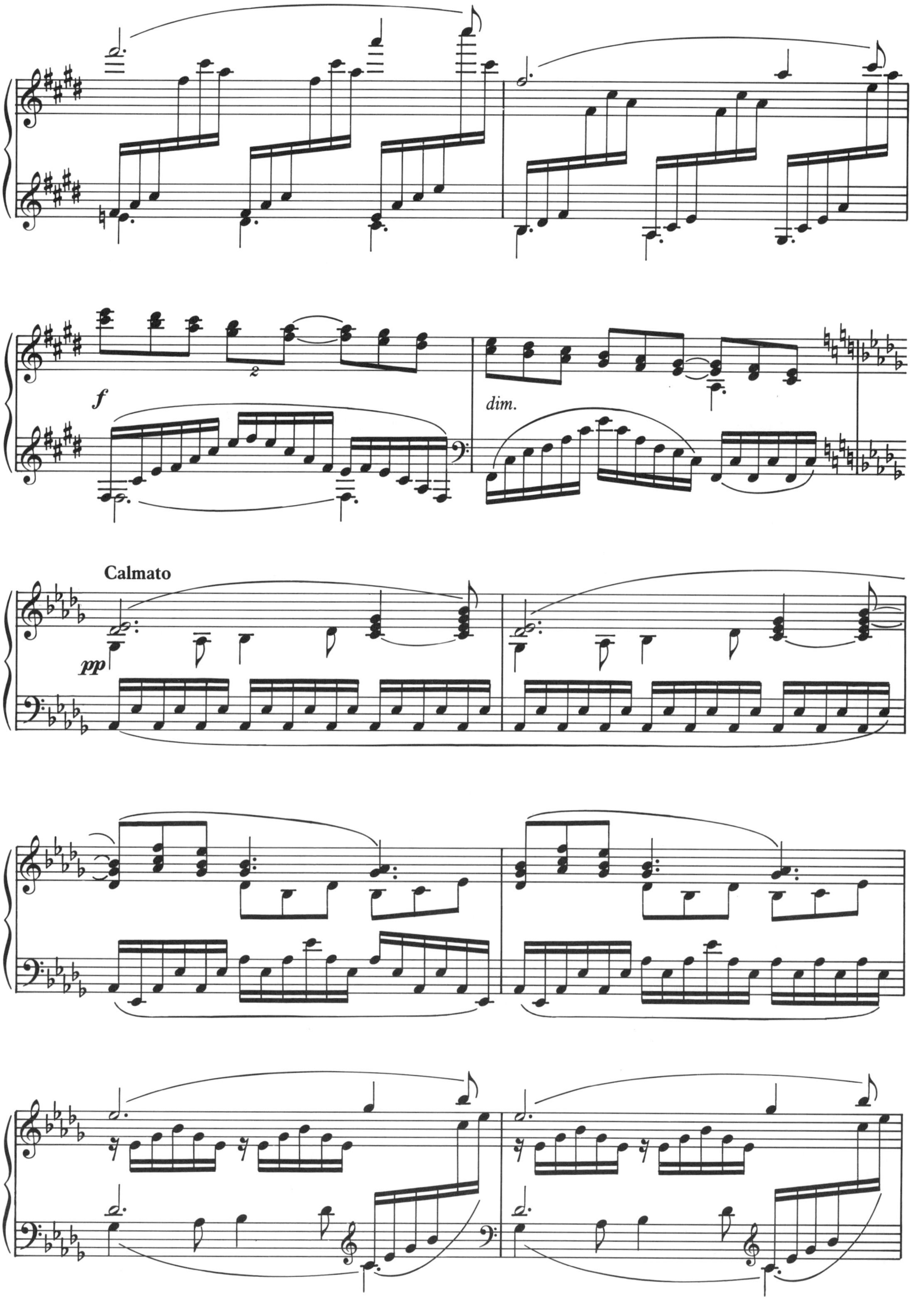
f
dim.
Calmato
pp

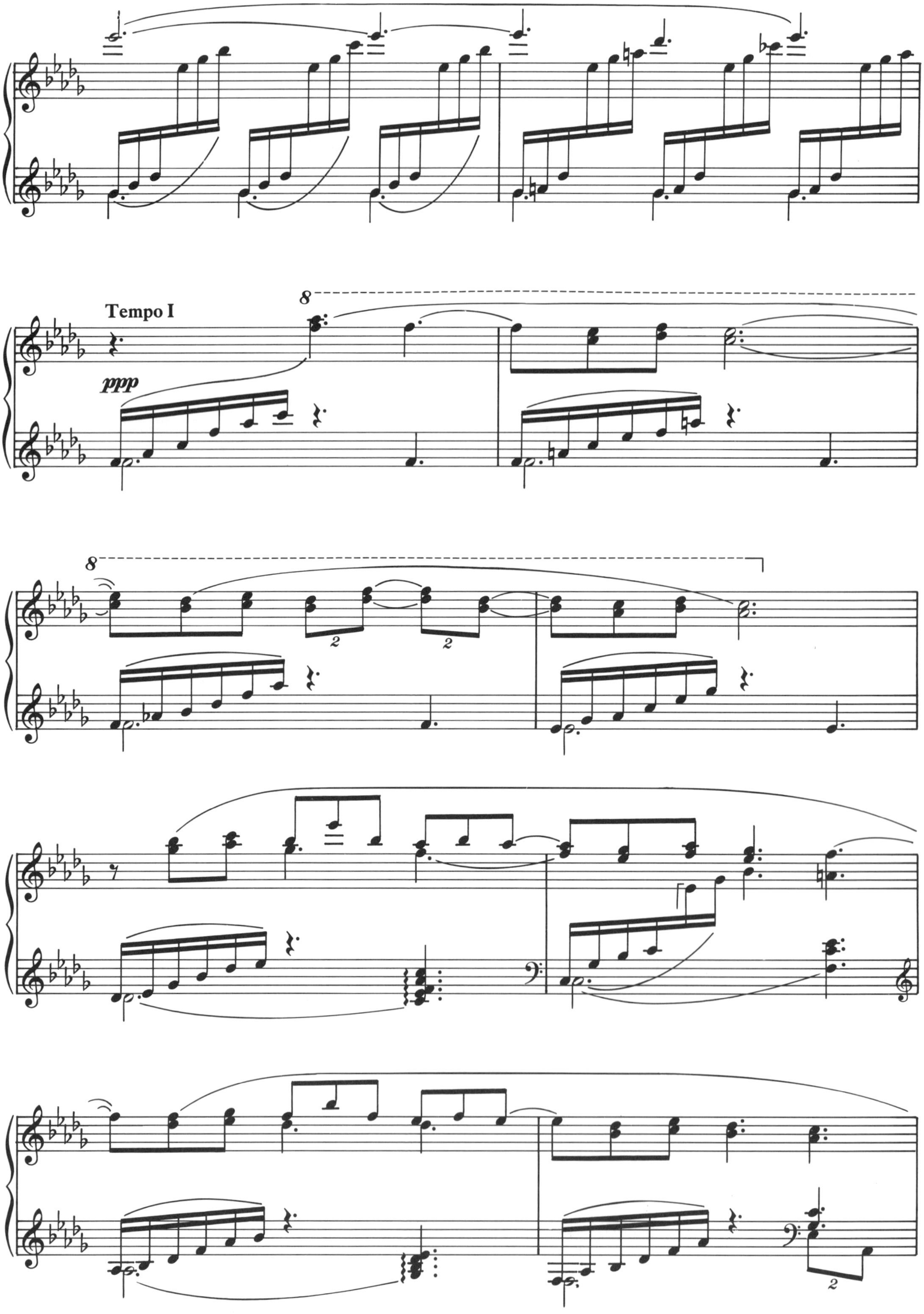
Tempo I
ppp
8
8
2
2
2

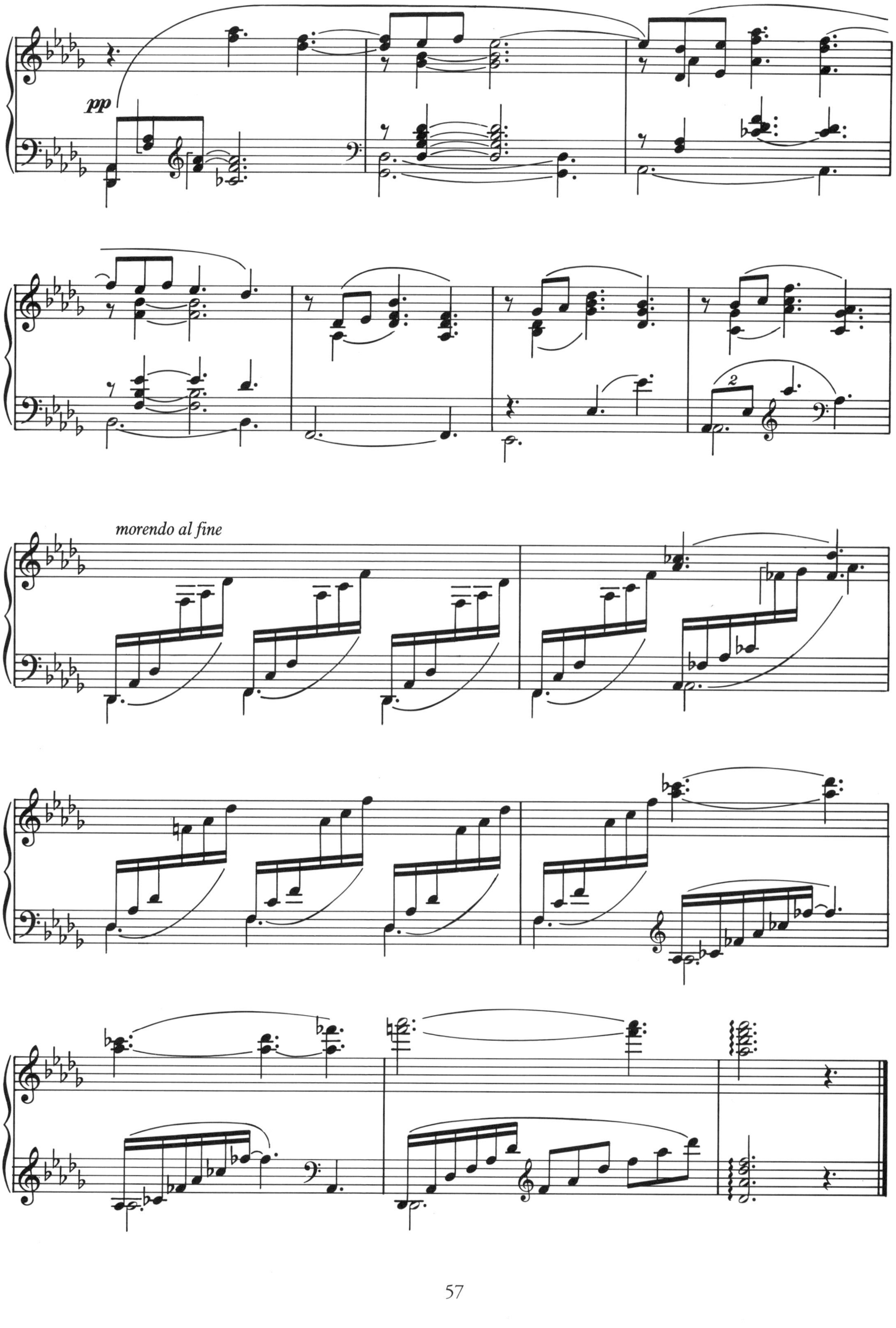
pp
2
morendo al fine

DREAMING

Robert Schumann (1810-1856)

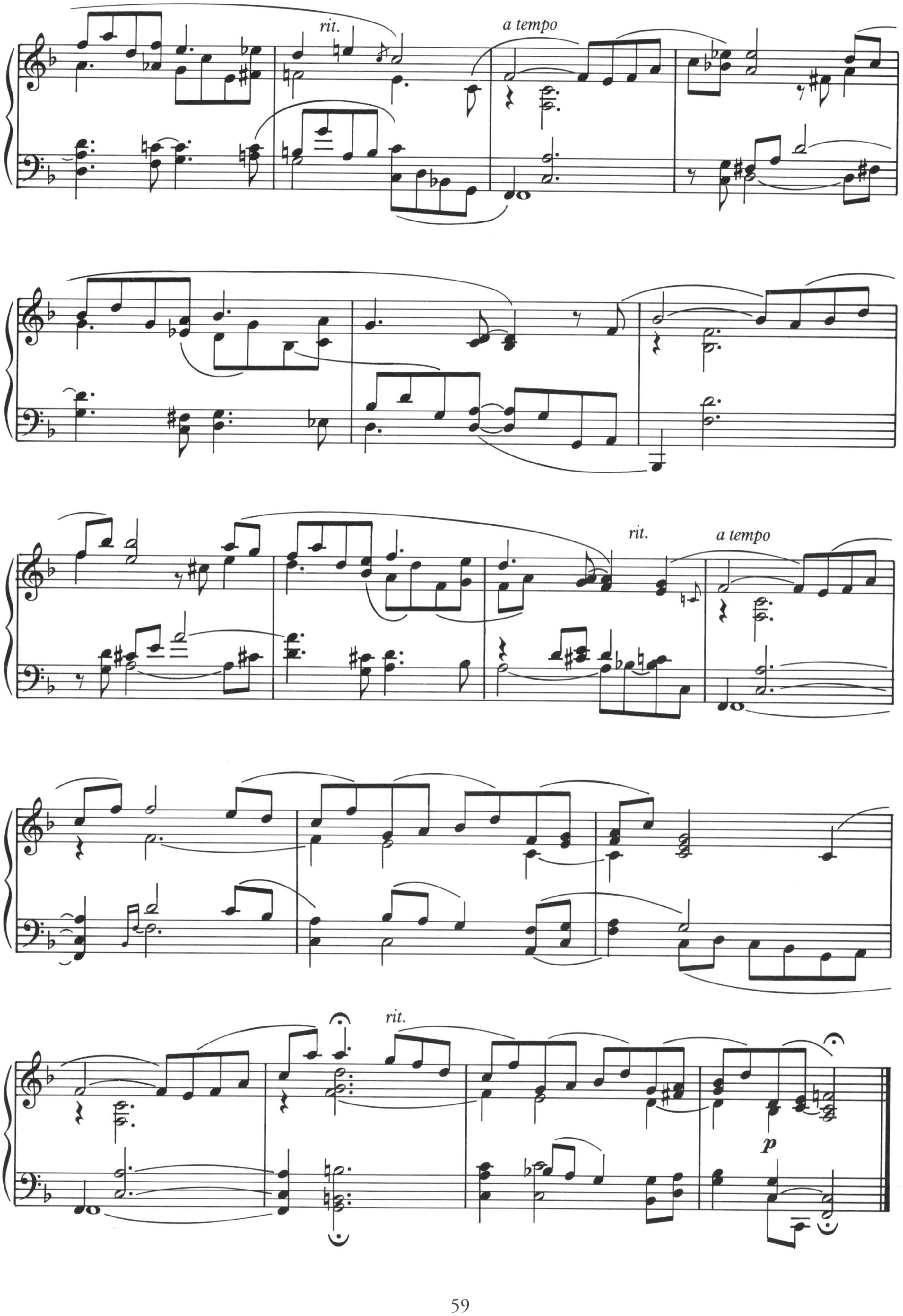
rit.
a tempo
rit.
a tempo
rit.
p

PRELUDE IN A

Frédéric Chopin (1810-1849)

ADAGIO from 'Moonlight Sonata'
Ludwig van Beethoven (1770-1827)

sempre **pp** *sempre legato*

© Copyright 1994 by Kevin Mayhew Ltd.
It is illegal to photocopy music.

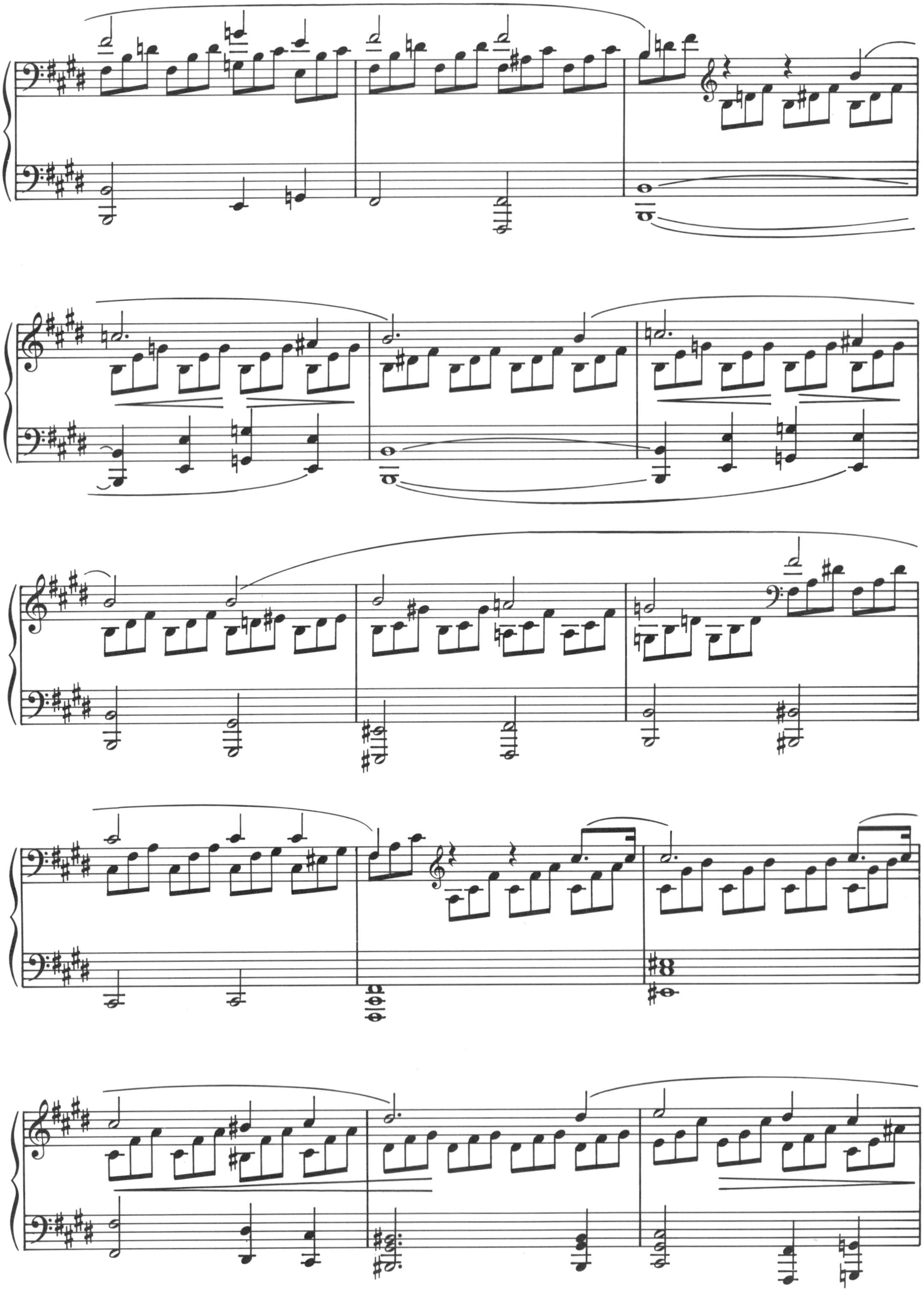

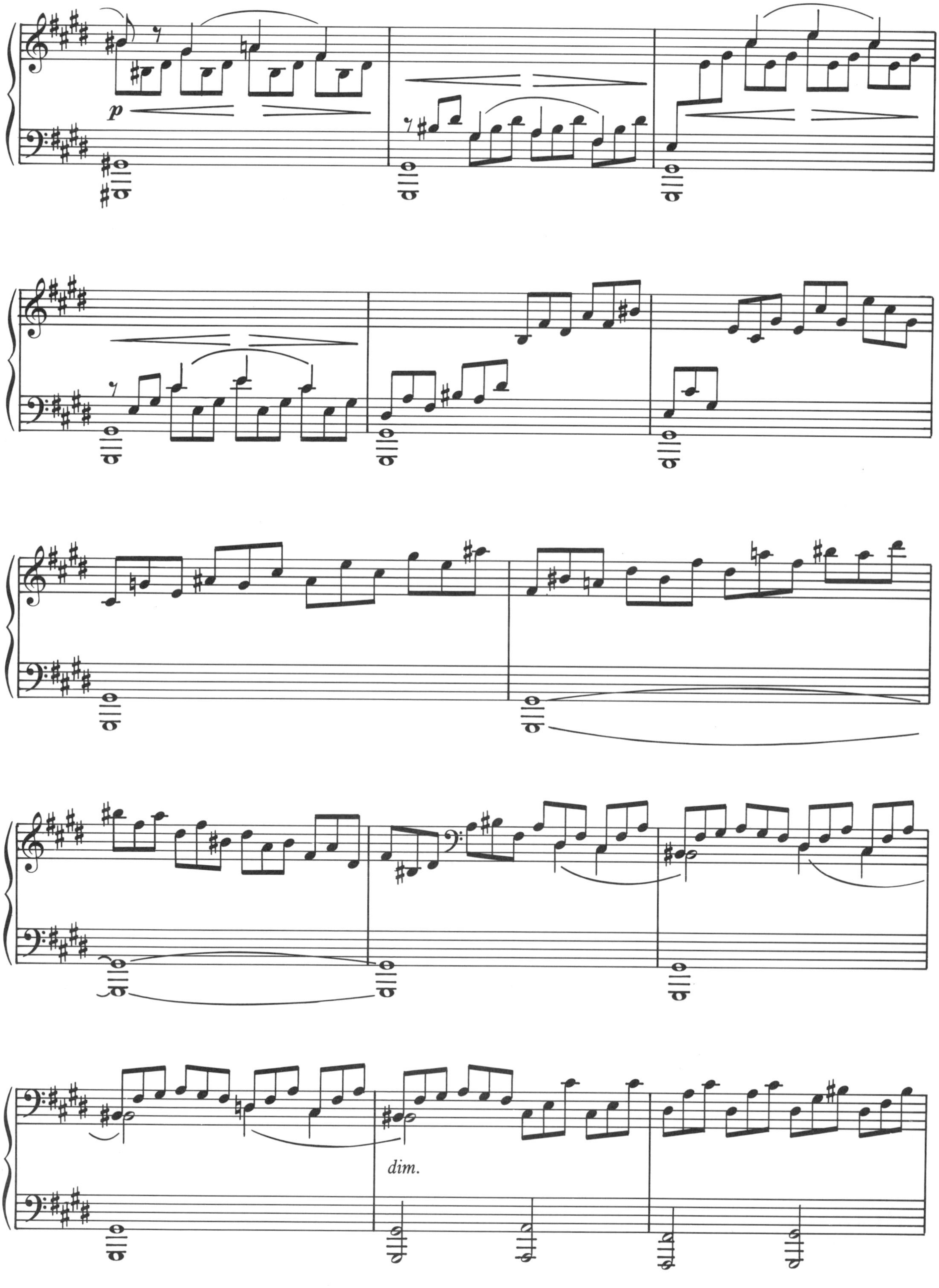
p
dim.

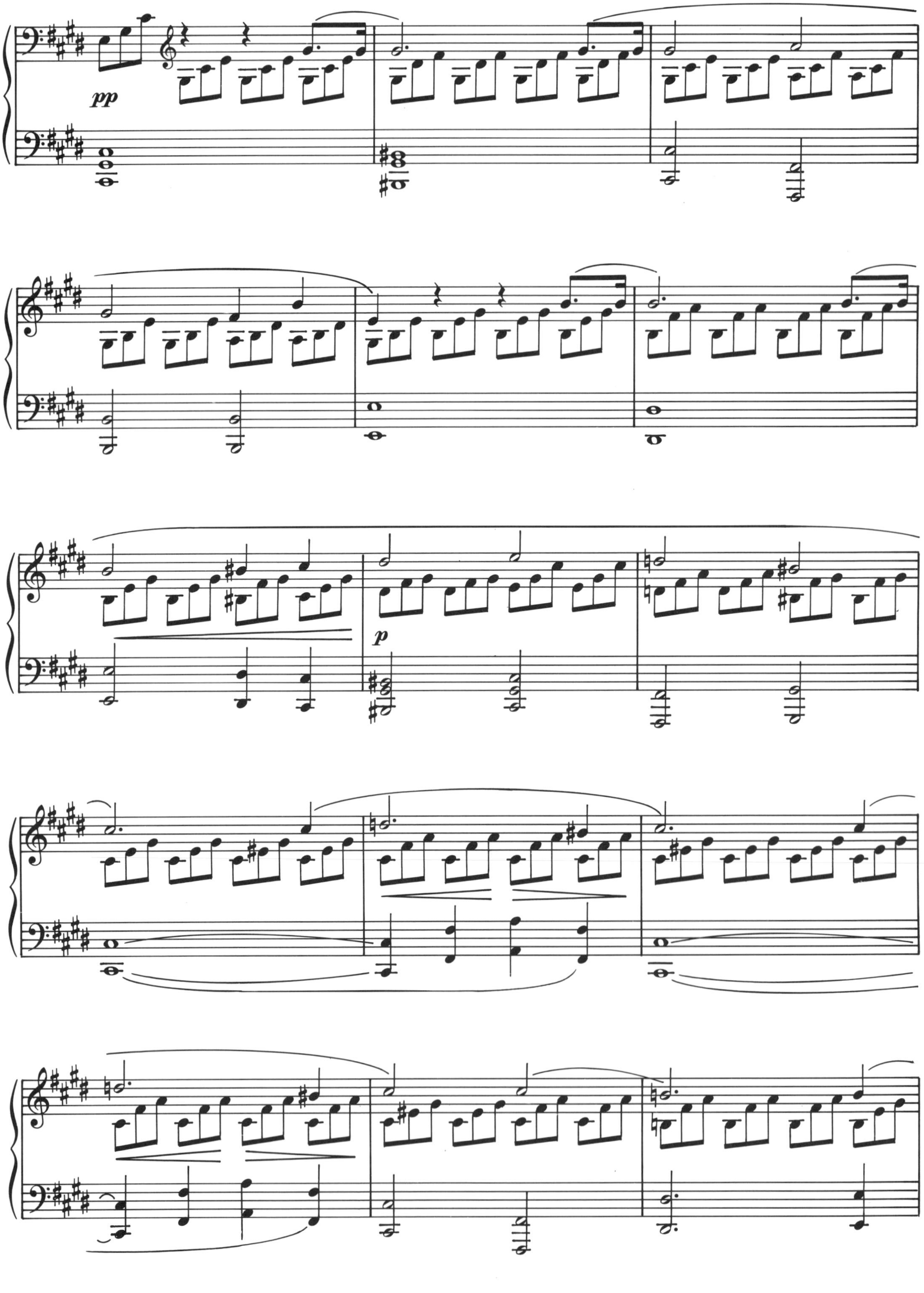
pp
p

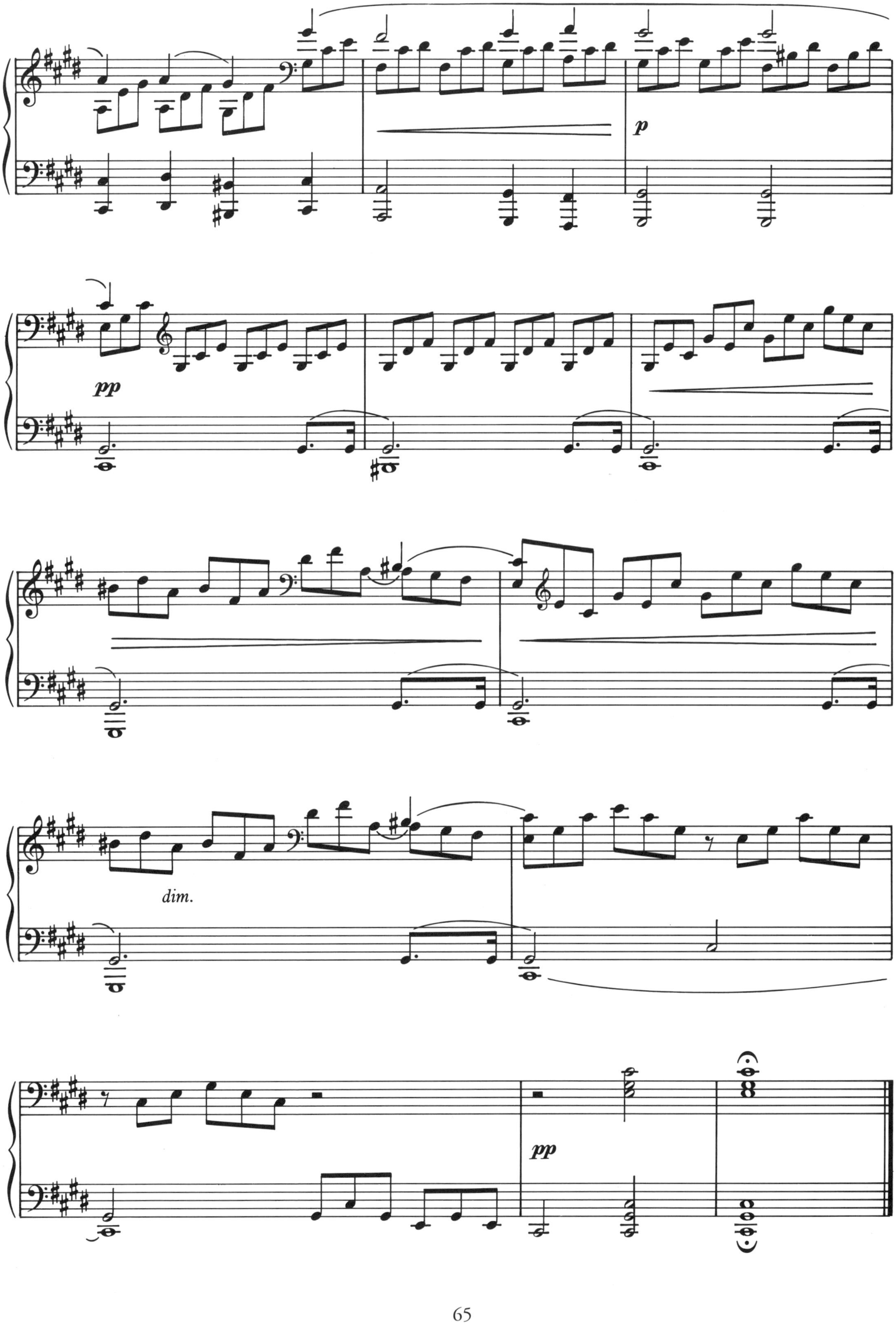
p
pp
dim.
pp

PRELUDE IN C MINOR
Johann Sebastian Bach (1685-1750)

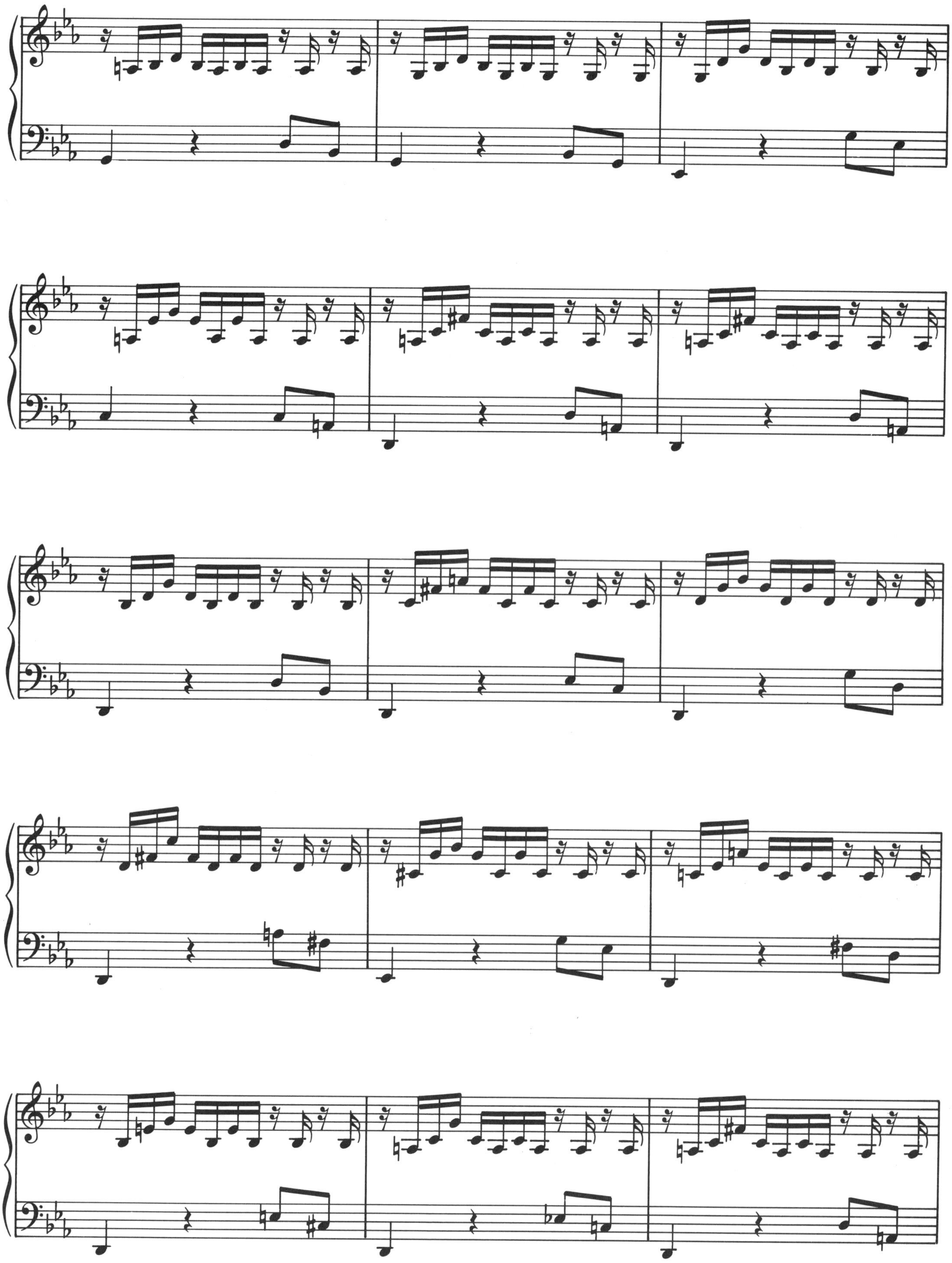

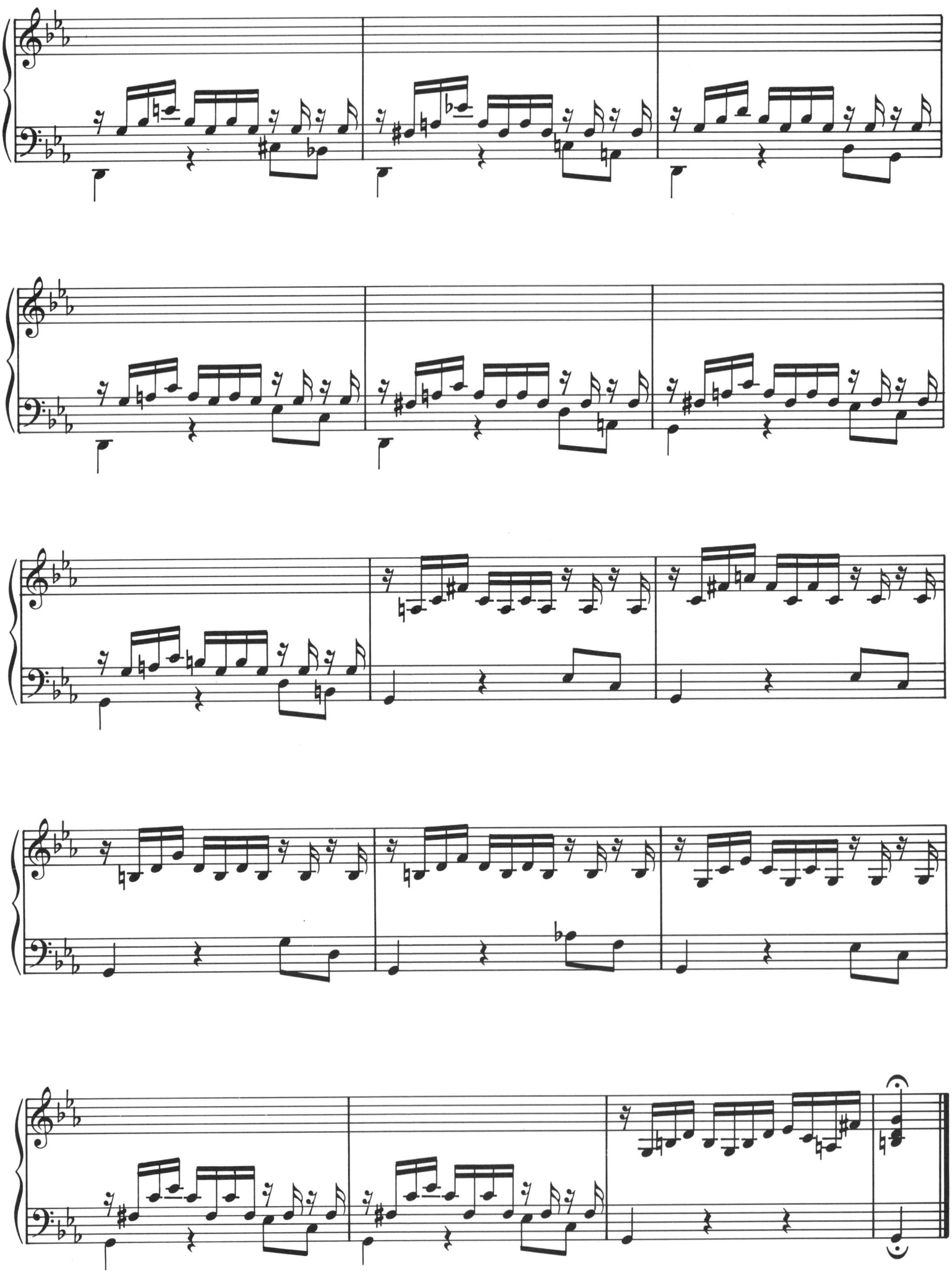

GYMNOPÉDIE I

Erik Satie (1866-1925)

Lent et douloureux

© Copyright 1994 by Kevin Mayhew Ltd.
It is illegal to photocopy music.

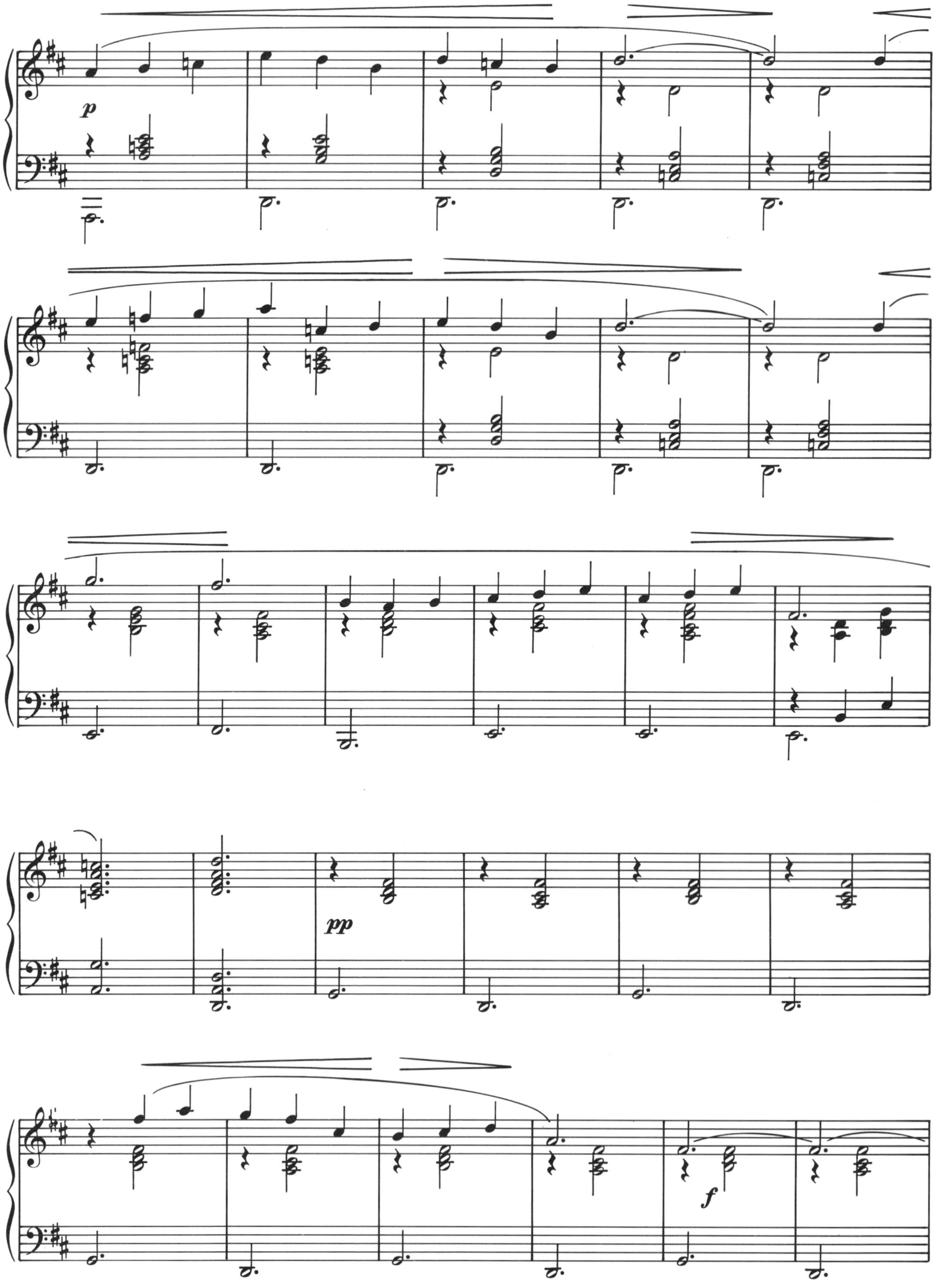
p
pp
f

71

REVERIE

Peter Ilyich Tchaikovsky (1840-1893)

73

THE GIRL WITH THE FLAXEN HAIR

Claude Debussy (1862-1918)

rit. *a tempo*
p *pp* *p*

rit. **Tempo I**
pp

rall.
murmuré
pp

perdendosi *pp*

PRELUDE IN E MINOR

Frédéric Chopin (1810-1849)

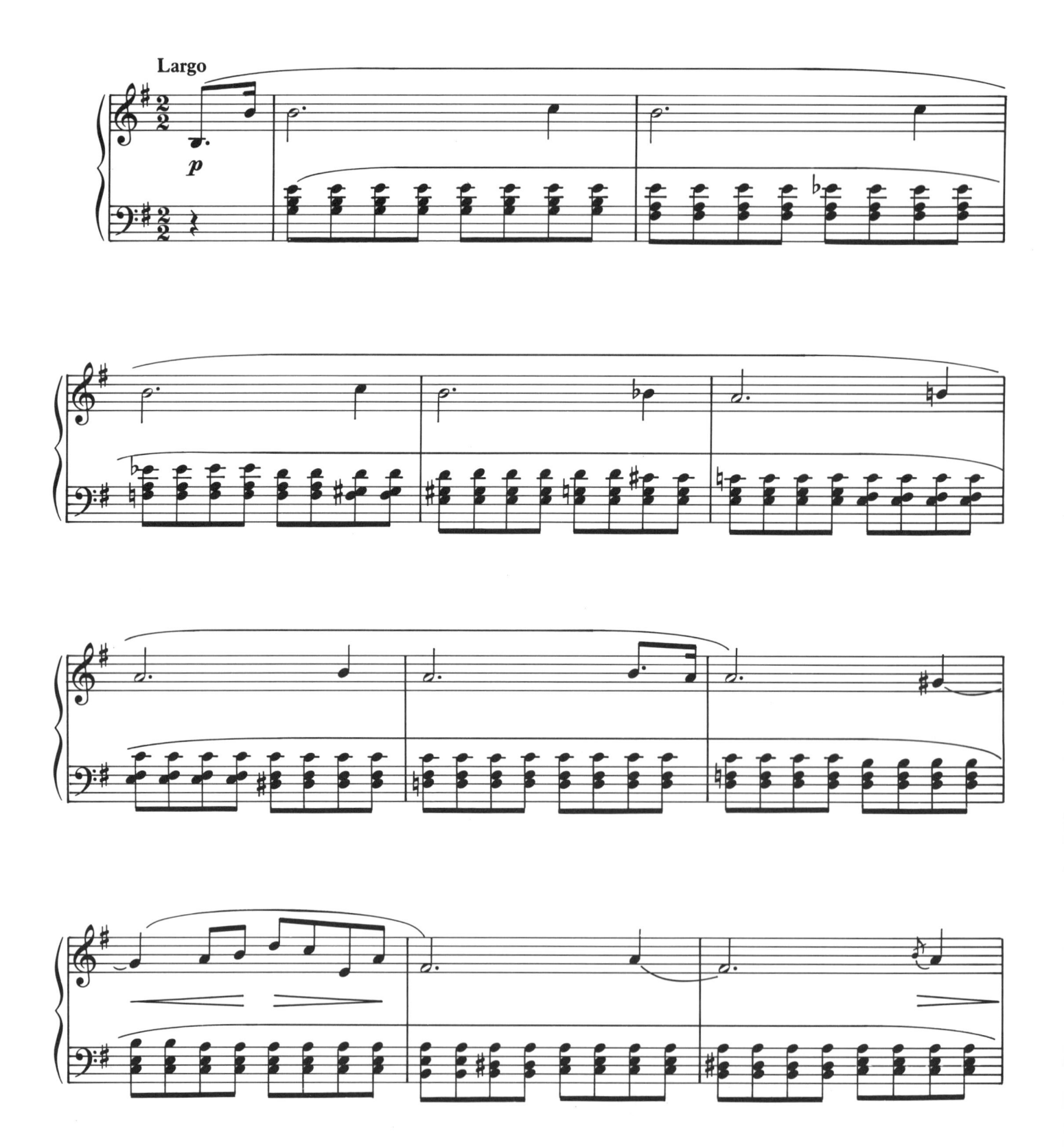

77

MOMENT MUSICAL No. 3

Franz Schubert (1797-1828)

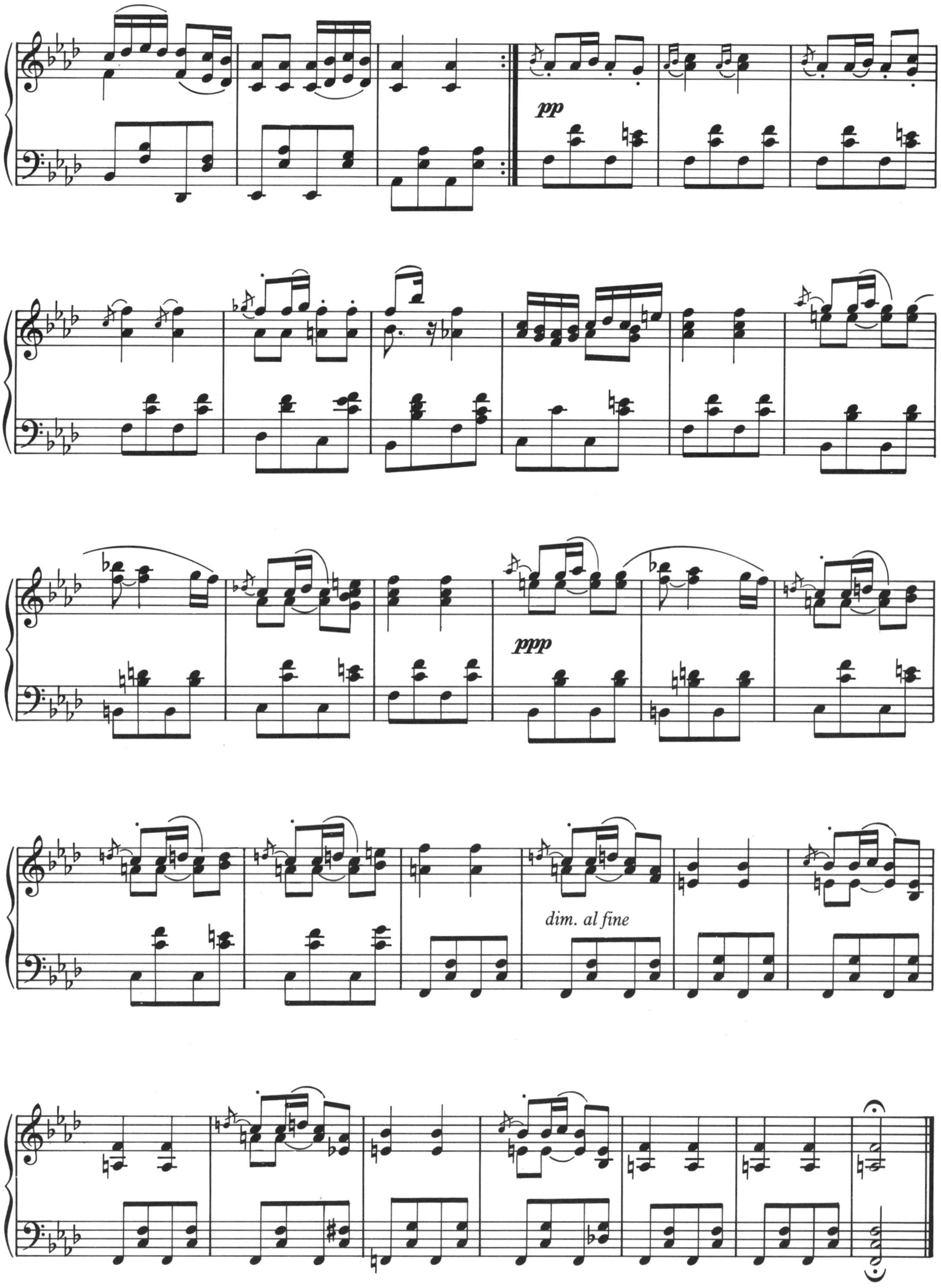
pp
ppp
dim. al fine